THE
101
GREATEST
BUSINESS PRINCIPLES
OF ALL TIME

THE
101
GREATEST
BUSINESS PRINCIPLES
OF ALL TIME

Edited by
Leslie Pockell
with
Adrienne Avila

WARNER
BUSINESS
BOOKS ™

NEW YORK   BOSTON

Warner Business Books

Time Warner Book Group
1271 Avenue of the Americas, New York, NY 10020
Visit our Web site at www.twbookmark.com

The Warner Business Books logo is a trademark of Warner Books.

Printed in the United States of America

First Edition: November 2004

10 9 8 7 6 5 4 3 2 1

ISBN: 0-446-57665-4

Book design and typesetting by Mada Design, Inc.

INTRODUCTION

◆

The world of business is no place for amateurs, and it usually takes years of running a gauntlet of mistaken assumptions and damaging missteps to become a true professional. The conventional MBA program provides all sorts of terminology and case studies that allow enthusiastic graduates to talk the talk of business, but like military basic training, it is no substitute for the realities of the battlefield. No matter how prepared you may feel, there will be many obstacles along the way, as there were for many of those whose words of wisdom are included here.

It is our hope that this book will serve as a kind of guide and inspire you as a mentor would, introducing concepts and revealing truths that every businessperson faces at some time in their career. To accomplish this we have searched for concise explications of the *fundamentals of business*, as well as essential principles of *investment*, *leadership*, *management*, *marketing*, and *success*, by some of the greatest entrepreneurs, managers, investors, and creative geniuses of all time, as well as eminent economists and theorists. In addition, some revelatory truths come from more unlikely sources, including the Bible, an advice columnist, and a country singer. To maximize the breadth of the insights provided here, we have included no more than one principle per person.

At first glance, some of the principles included here may seem simplistic rather than profound; others may appear to overlap, or to be contradictory. Still others may appear facetious. But it is our belief that taken together they will help to inculcate some basic realities that are valid for both business and life as a whole. The world of business, like the world at large, is not something that is controllable by power, wealth, or force of will alone; while useful guidelines certainly exist, there are no magic formulas. After all, business ultimately involves people, each of whom has needs, desires, strengths, and weaknesses. It is those who are best able to communicate with, empathize with, and inspire their colleagues and their customers, and to mobilize their strengths and minimize their weaknesses, who are most likely to succeed in the world of business.

We would like to think our editor, Rick Wolff, for initiating and guiding this project, and Jamie Raab for her enthusiastic support. Patricia Canseco also provided essential editorial contributions.

Leslie Pockell
Adrienne Avila

CONTENTS

◆

Part 1

The Fundamentals

◆

Buy cheap, sell dear.

◆

John Greenleaf Whittier

Only a fool holds out for top dollar.

◆

Joseph P. Kennedy

Cut your losses, and let your profits run.

◆

Anonymous

The engine which drives Enterprise is not Thrift, but Profit.

◆

John Maynard Keynes

There are three secrets to real estate:

Location, location, location.

◆

William Dillard

If you can run one business well,
you can run any business well.

◆

Richard Branson

For unto every one that hath shall be given, and he shall have abundance: but from him that hath not shall be taken away even that which he hath.

◆

Matthew 25:29

Every individual . . . intends only his own gain, and he is in this, as in many other cases, led by an invisible hand to promote an end which was no part of his intention. Nor is it always the worse for the society that it was no part of it. By pursuing his own interest he frequently promotes that of the society more effectually than when he really intends to promote it.

◆

Adam Smith, *The Wealth of Nations*

PARETO'S PRINCIPLE

Twenty percent of your products will
generate eighty percent of your income.
Twenty percent of your income will require
eighty percent of your resources.

◆

Vilfredo Pareto

There was an old owl lived in an oak,

The more he heard, the less he spoke;

The less he spoke, the more he heard.

O, if men were like that wise old bird.

Punch

A dinner lubricates business.

◆

William Scott, Baron Stowell

PARKINSON'S LAW

Work expands so as to fill the time
available for its completion.

◆

C. Northcote Parkinson

THE PETER PRINCIPLE

In a hierarchical organization every employee
tends to rise to his level of incompetence.

Lawrence Peter

MURPHY'S LAW

If there are two or more ways to do
something, and one of those ways can result
in catastrophe, then someone will do it.

◆

Edward A. Murphy, Jr.

Do it fast, do it right, do it cheap.
Pick two.

◆

Anonymous

A camel is a horse put together
by a committee.

◆

Anonymous

One may smile, and smile, and be a villain.

◆

William Shakespeare, *Hamlet*

Don't be afraid of going slowly.

Only be afraid of standing still.

◆

Anonymous

Trust yourself. You know more than you think you do.

◆

Benjamin Spock

Don't be afraid to take a big step
when one is indicated. You can't cross
a chasm in two small steps.

◆

David Lloyd George

You can gain strength, courage, and confidence by every experience in which you really stop to look fear in the face. . . . You must do the thing which you think you cannot do.

◆

Eleanor Roosevelt

Power can be taken, but not given.
The process of the taking is
empowerment in itself.

◆

Gloria Steinem

When people go to work, they shouldn't have to leave their hearts at home.

◆

Betty Bender

Be nice to people on your way up because you might meet them on your way down.

◆

Alexandre Dumas *père*

Part 2

Investment

At the turn of the twentieth century, two men were walking along the East River waterfront, not far from the headquarters of the New York Stock Exchange. One man pointed to the array of elegant sailing boats tied to the dock and said, "Those yachts belong to the celebrated stockbrokers on Wall Street." The other man looked at him and asked, "Where are all the customers' yachts?"

Fred Schwed, Jr.

Our favorite holding period is forever.

◆

Warren Buffett

It is not how much you make that counts,
but how much money you keep.

◆

Robert Kiyosaki

Make no investments without a
full acquaintance with their nature and
condition; and select such investments
as have intrinsic value.

◆

Benjamin Franklin

Never invest your money in anything that eats or needs repairing.

Billy Rose

The market is a place set apart where
men may deceive each other.

◆

Diogenes Laertius

Bulls make money. Bears make money.
Pigs get slaughtered.

◆

Anonymous

Business? It's quite simple.
It's other people's money.

◆

Alexandre Dumas *fils*

Sometimes your best investments are the ones you don't make.

◆

Donald Trump, quoting W. H. Auden

Part 3

Leadership

No man will make a great leader
who wants to do it all himself, or to get
all the credit for doing it.

◆

Andrew Carnegie

The difference between a boss and a leader:

A boss says, "Go!"

A leader says, "Let's go!"

◆

E. M. Kelly

You don't lead by hitting people over the head . . . that's assault, not leadership.

◆

Dwight D. Eisenhower

The key to successful leadership today is influence, not authority.

Kenneth Blanchard

No person can be a great leader

unless he takes genuine joy in the

successes of those under him.

◆

Anonymous

I praise loudly and I blame softly.

◆

Catherine the Great

People are persuaded by reason, but moved by emotion; [the leader] must both persuade them and move them.

◆

Richard M. Nixon

As we look ahead into the next century,

leaders will be those who empower others.

Bill Gates

Outstanding leaders go out of their way
to boost the self-esteem of their personnel.
If people believe in themselves, it's amazing
what they can accomplish.

◆

Sam Walton

Charisma is the gift from above where a leader knows from inside himself what to do.

Max Weber

Failing organizations are usually
overmanaged and underled.

◆

Warren G. Bennis

For if the trumpet give an uncertain sound,
who shall prepare himself to the battle?

◆

I Corinthians, 14:8

Now the general who wins a battle makes many calculations before the battle is fought. The general who loses a battle makes only a few calculations beforehand. In this way many calculations lead to victory, and few calculations to defeat.

Sun-tzu, *The Art of War*

You gotta be first, best, or different.

Loretta Lynn

Lead, follow, or get the hell out of the way.

◆

George Steinbrenner

Carry a bottle of water in one hand, fertilizer in the other. Put water on the employees who are seeds, and watch the garden grow. You'll get some weeds. Cut out the weeds and eventually build a gorgeous garden.

Jack Welch

Part 4

Management

A good manager is a man who isn't worried about his own career but rather the careers of those who work for him. My advice: Don't worry about yourself. Take care of those who work for you and you'll float to greatness on their achievements.

◆

H. S. M. Burns

There is no substitute for accurate knowledge. Know yourself, know your business, know your men.

◆

Randall Jacobs

Use the right tool for the job.

Let the tool do the work.

Take care of your tools.

◆

Stanley E. West

Surround yourself with the best people
you can find, delegate authority,
and don't interfere.

Ronald Reagan

Make every decision as if you owned the whole company.

Robert Townsend

Never mistake activity for achievement.

John Wooden

The ideas that come out of most brainstorming sessions are usually superficial, trivial, and not very original. They are rarely useful. The process, however, seems to make uncreative people feel that they are making innovative contributions and that others are listening to them.

◆

A. Harvey Block

It is amazing what can be accomplished
when nobody cares about who
gets the credit.

◆

Robert Yates

Compromise is the art of dividing a cake

in such a way that everyone believes

that he has got the biggest piece.

◆

Ludwig Erhard

Behavior in offices often resembles the wild. For example, when a lion is stalking its prey, herd animals are restless and prone to stampede, but after the lion makes its kill, the herd animals soon return to grazing peacefully.

◆

Anonymous

Competition between individuals sets one against the other and undermines morale, but competition between organizations builds morale and encourages creativity.

◆

George Washington Allston

Avoid mushroom management
(keeping your employees in the dark
and covered in horseshit).

◆

Anonymous

Tell me and I'll forget,

show me and I may remember,

involve me and I'll understand.

◆

Chinese proverb

Surround yourself with skeptics,
not true believers who tell you what you
want to hear. Demand that your gatekeepers
be truth tellers, too, and that they push back
whenever they see a lapse in judgment
on your part.

◆

David F. D'Alessandro

Any manager who can't get along
with a .400 hitter is crazy.

◆

Joe McCarthy

Business, more than any other occupation,

is a continual dealing with the future;

it is a continual calculation,

an instinctive exercise in foresight.

◆

Henry R. Luce

First-rate people hire first-rate people;
second-rate people hire third-rate people.

◆

Leo Rosten

It's not what you pay a man
but what he costs you that counts.

Will Rogers

The budget evolved from a management tool into an obstacle to management.

◆

Frank Carlucci

Part 5

Marketing

The customer is god.

◆

Japanese proverb

Above all, we wish to avoid having a dissatisfied customer. We consider our customers a part of our organization, and we want them to feel free to make any criticism they see fit in regard to our merchandise or service. Sell practical, tested merchandise at reasonable profit, treat your customers like human beings—and they will always come back.

L. L. Bean

Profit in business comes from repeat customers, customers that boast about your project or service, and that bring friends with them.

◆

W. Edwards Deming

Many a small thing has been made large
by the right kind of advertising.

◆

Mark Twain

Early to bed, early to rise.

Work like hell and advertise.

◆

Ted Turner

UNIQUE SELLING PROPOSITION

• Each advertisement must make a proposition to the consumer.

• The proposition must be one that the competition either cannot or does not offer. It must be unique—either a uniqueness of the brand or a claim not otherwise made in that particular field of advertising.

• The proposition must be so strong that it can move the mass millions.

Rosser Reeves

The consumer isn't a moron.

She is your wife.

◆

David Ogilvy

Anybody can cut prices, but it takes brains to produce a better article.

◆

P. D. Armour

Part 6

Success

Trust your hunches. They're usually based on facts filed away just below the conscious level.

◆

Dr. Joyce Brothers

Opportunity is missed by most people because it comes dressed in overalls and looks like work.

◆

Thomas Edison

There is no security on this earth.
There is only opportunity.

◆

Douglas MacArthur

Whenever you are asked if you can do a job, tell 'em, "Certainly, I can!" Then get busy and find out how to do it.

◆

Theodore Roosevelt

The difference between a successful person and others is not a lack of strength, not a lack of knowledge, but rather a lack of will.

◆

Vince Lombardi

If you want something done, ask a busy person to do it. The more things you do, the more you can do.

◆

Lucille Ball

When I was young I observed that
nine out of ten things I did were failures,
so I did ten times more work.

◆

George Bernard Shaw

I don't measure a man's success by how high he climbs, but how high he bounces when he hits bottom.

◆

George S. Patton

I was told over and over again that I would never be successful, that I was not going to be competitive and the technique was simply not going to work. All I could do was shrug and say, "We'll just have to see."

◆

Dick Fosbury, whose revolutionary high-jumping technique enabled him to win an Olympic gold medal in 1968

People of mediocre ability sometimes achieve outstanding success because they don't know when to quit. Most men succeed because they are determined to.

George E. Allen

Whenever an individual decides that success has been attained, progress stops.

◆

Thomas J. Watson, Jr.

Some people believe that holding on
and hanging in there are signs of great
strength. However, there are times when it
takes much more strength to know
when to let go—and then to do it.

Ann Landers

There is nothing so useless as doing efficiently that which should not be done at all.

◆

Peter Drucker

It is awfully important to know what is
and what is not your business.

◆

Gertrude Stein

The biggest mistake we could ever make

in our lives is to think we work

for anybody but ourselves.

◆

Brian Tracy

I have found that being honest is the best technique I can use. Right up front, tell people what you're trying to accomplish and what you're willing to sacrifice to accomplish it.

Lee Iacocca

The secret of life is honesty and fair
dealing. . . . If you can fake that,
you've got it made.

◆

Groucho Marx

The essence of success is that it is never necessary to think of a new idea oneself. It is far better to wait until somebody else does it, and then to copy him in every detail, except his mistakes.

◆

Aubrey Menen

A memorandum is written not to inform the reader, but to protect the writer.

◆

Dean Acheson

Private victories precede public victories.

Stephen R. Covey

One of the symptoms of an approaching
nervous breakdown is the belief that one's
work is terribly important.

◆

Bertrand Russell

Don't be irreplaceable—if you can't be replaced, you can't be promoted.

◆

Dilbert (Scott Adams)

Conducting your business in a socially responsible way is good business. It means that you can attract better employees and that customers will know what you stand for and like you for it.

◆

M. Anthony Burns

I don't know the key to success, but the key to failure is trying to please everybody.

Bill Cosby

It's a poor workman who blames his tools.

Anonymous

Also edited by Leslie Pockell

The 100 Best Poems of All Time
The 13 Best Horror Stories of All Time

with Adrienne Avila

The 100 Best Love Poems of All Time
Everything I've Learned: 100 Great Principles to Live By